D1384891

SCIENCE WIDE OPEN

Women in Physics

Written by Mary Wissinger
Illustrated by Danielle Pioli

Created and Edited by John J. Coveyou

Why do things fall down?

What an excellent question! Things fall down to the ground because the Earth pulls them toward itself. That pull is called gravity.

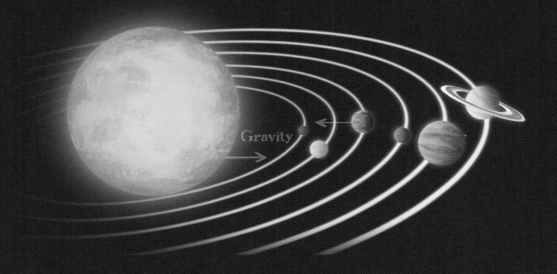

Gravity

Émilie du Châtelet was also curious about gravity, but finding answers wasn't easy.

People talked about big ideas in cafes, but back then only men were allowed. Émilie dressed in men's clothing so she could join the conversation.

To make it tougher, the best book on things like gravity - Newton's Principia - was written in a foreign language.

But that didn't stop a brave woman like Émilie.

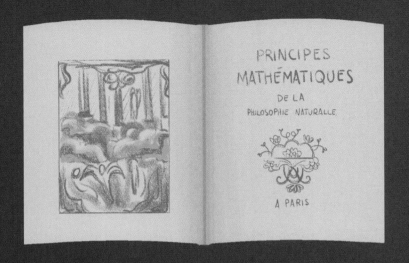

Émilie spent four years translating the entire book into her language. Her research and experiments helped her create equations and form new ideas about gravity. She got people around the world excited about physics, and her work inspired future scientists like Einstein.

(France, 1706 - 1749)

That sounds important. But what's physics?

So glad you asked! Physics is the study of how and why everything in the universe moves and works. Physics helps us explain how birds can fly, or why water freezes when it's cold and turns into steam when it's hot.

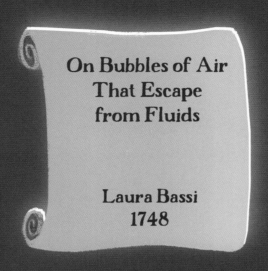

On Bubbles of Air
That Escape
from Fluids

Laura Bassi
1748

Laura Bassi could tell you all about those things because she was the first woman in the world to be a professor of physics. She ran many experiments on things like bubbles, water, and fire.

Her house was full of scientific equipment, and she even gave physics lessons in her home! She loved studying force - that's the push or pull on things in the universe.

(Italy, 1711–1778)

Can I catch force?

No, we can't catch force or even see it. Force is invisible.

But how can we study something we can't see?

Even though we can't see force, we can see and feel what force does. A ball sitting in the grass stays still until you kick it. The force from the ball pushes your foot, but the force from your kick is stronger and sends the ball sailing... until the force of gravity pulls it back down to Earth.

Physicists study lots of things we can't see. They start with a question and a possible answer – that's a hypothesis. Then they run experiments and observe the results to see if they were correct.

Radioactive atom

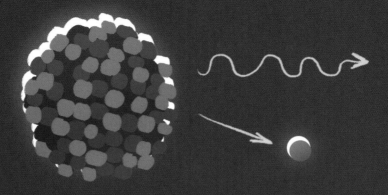

Marie Curie was famous for her experiments with radioactivity, a type of energy that can move in invisible waves.

Marie won a Nobel Prize for her work - the first one ever awarded to a woman. She kept experimenting and won another Nobel Prize for discovering two new radioactive elements: Radium and Polonium.

(Poland and France, 1867 - 1934)

What are elements?

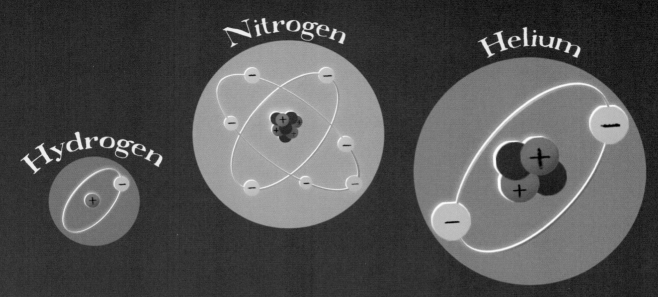

Hydrogen

Nitrogen

Helium

An element is the name given to each type of atom.

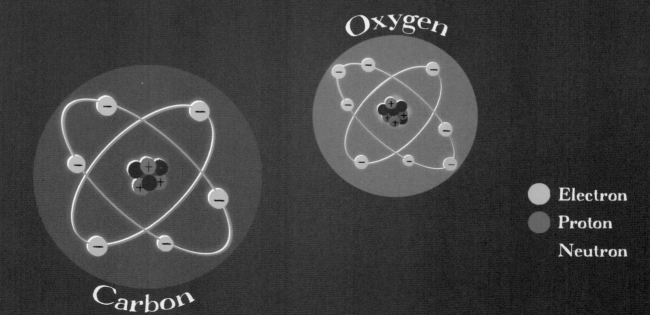

Oxygen

Carbon

Electron
Proton
Neutron

You can think of atoms as tiny building blocks that make up everything in the universe.

Marie and her daughter Irene Joliot-Curie dedicated their lives to studying elements and radioactivity.

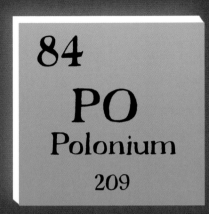

84

PO

Polonium

209

Sometimes Irene was so focused that she forgot to say hello to other lab workers. She spent years conducting experiments, especially with the element Polonium that her mom discovered.

Irene's hard work paid off though, and she won a Nobel Prize for research, too! Marie and Irene were the first parent and child to both win Nobel Prizes for their discoveries.

I want to discover something!

You can!

We're always learning new things about how the universe works, but it takes patience and lots of hard work to make discoveries.

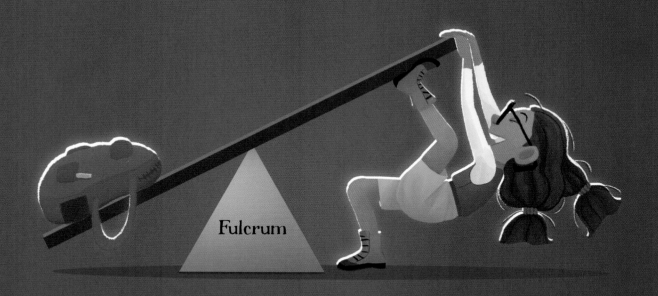

Just look at Chien-Shiung Wu. Her name meant "Courageous Hero," but she was more than that. She fearlessly asked big questions and ran complex experiments to find the answers.

Chien-Shiung loved doing careful work and making observations. She helped make a discovery that surprised the world.

China and United States, 1912 - 1997)

Cool! How'd she do that?

Well, people thought they knew exactly what happened when atoms fall apart, but they were wrong. Chien-Shiung's experiment showed something completely different! Her results were so amazing that it changed the way people looked at physics. It was like she dropped something up instead of down!

That's really incredible!

But...we know that things fall to the ground, because of gravity.

You're right.

But a scientist like you can double check by making a hypothesis, conducting an experiment, and observing the results. That way, you can make your own discoveries, too!

Can you find...?

Émilie du Châtelet (EM-i-lee du SHAH-tuh-leh)

Laura Bassi (LAH-rah BAH-see)

Marie Curie (MAH-ree CURE-ee)

Irene Joliot-Curie (EE-ren ZHOH-lee-oh CURE-ee)

Chien-Shiung Wu (chyen shyung woo)

Glossary

MASS: A measure of how much a thing resists being moved.

MATTER: Anything that takes up space and has mass.

ENERGY: The ability to do work.

PHYSICS: The study of matter, energy, and how they interact.

FORCE: The push or pull on a thing when it interacts with another thing.

GRAVITY: A force that attracts ALL objects toward each other. This force gets bigger as the objects get bigger, which is why our bodies feel the force of gravity from the earth, but not from a spoon or apple.

ATOMS: Atoms are like the building blocks that put together our universe. Different kinds of atoms are made by combining different numbers of protons, neutrons, and electrons.

ELEMENT: A basic substance made of one type of atom that usually cannot be separated into simpler substances.

Glossary

RADIOACTIVITY: The particles and energy an atom gives off when its nucleus is broken apart.

X-RAY: Invisible rays of high energy and short wavelength that can pass through things and make it possible to see inside them.

OBSERVATION: Using our senses to collect information about the world.

RESEARCH: To investigate and study something in order to learn new things about it.

HYPOTHESIS: A scientific guess that a scientist makes to explain something they think is true or think will happen.

EXPERIMENT: A test to collect information about the world to see if a hypothesis is correct.

NOBEL PRIZE: An award given for amazing work in chemistry, physics, physiology or medicine, literature or economics. Being given a Nobel Prize is one of the greatest honors a scientist can get!

Bibliography

Hypatia's Heritage: A History of Women in Science from Antiquity through the Nineteenth Century by Margaret Alic (Beacon Press, 1986).

Magnificent Minds: 16 Pioneering Women in Science & Medicine by Pendred E. Noyce (Tumblehome Learning, Inc., 2015).

Notable Women Scientists edited by Pamela Proffitt. (Gale Group, 1999).

Super Women in Science by Kelly Di Domenico (Second Story Press, 2002).

Remarkable Minds: 17 More Pioneering Women in Science & Medicine by Pendred E. Noyce (Tumblehome Learning, Inc., 2015).

Written by Mary Wissinger

Illustrated by Danielle Pioli

Created and Edited by John J. Coveyou

Science Wide Open and the distinctive logo and characters are a trademark of Genius Games, LLC. in St. Louis, MO.

Manufactured in the USA.

ISBN 978-1-945779-11-4

gotgeniusgames.com